Spooky Spots

SPOOKY SCHOOLS & LIBRARIES

ELSIE OLSON

Big Buddy Books

An Imprint of Abdo Publishing
abdobooks.com

abdobooks.com

Published by Abdo Publishing, a division of ABDO, PO Box 398166, Minneapolis, Minnesota 55439.

Printed in the United States of America, North Mankato, Minnesota
052020
092020

Design: Sarah DeYoung, Mighty Media, Inc.
Production: Mighty Media, Inc.
Editor: Liz Salzmann

Cover Photograph: Shutterstock Images
Interior Photographs: Courtesy of the Willard Library Archives, pp. 12-13; Espresso Addict/Wikimedia Commons, p. 7 (Combermere Abbey); George Chriss/Wikimedia Commons, pp. 6 (Penn State), 25; Nyttend/Wikimedia Commons, pp. 6 (Willard Library), 10-11; Sam Felder/Flickr, pp. 6 (Peoria Library), 23; Shutterstock Images, pp. 4-5, 6, 7, 15, 17, 19, 20, 21, 26, 27, 28 (all), 29 (all); Topham Partners LLP/Alamy, p. 9
Design Elements: Shutterstock Images

Library of Congress Control Number: 2020932465

Publisher's Cataloging-in-Publication Data
Names: Olson, Elsie, author.
Title: Spooky schools & libraries / by Elsie Olson
Description: Minneapolis, Minnesota : Abdo Publishing, 2021 | Series: Spooky spots | Includes online resources and index
Identifiers: ISBN 9781532193354 (lib. bdg.) | ISBN 9781098211998 (ebook)
Subjects: LCSH: Haunted places--Juvenile literature. | Ghosts--Juvenile literature. | Schools--Juvenile literature. | Libraries--Juvenile literature. | Spirits--Juvenile literature.
Classification: DDC 133.12--dc23

CONTENTS

Haunted Schools and Libraries 4
World's Spookiest Schools and Libraries 6
Combermere Abbey Library 8
Willard Library 10
The Dow Hill Schools 14
CSU Channel Islands 16
University of St. Andrews 18
Peoria Public Library 22
Penn State 24
State Library of Victoria 26
Spooky or Science? 28
Glossary 30
Online Resources 31
Index 32

HAUNTED SCHOOLS AND LIBRARIES

Do you believe there are ghosts among us? Many people do. Whether you're a believer or not, schools and libraries are some of the spookiest spots around!

Get ready to **explore** some of the most haunted schools and libraries on Earth. Walk past shelves of dusty books. Wander through empty school hallways and gyms. But look out! You may not be alone.

Many people believe that the older a school or library is, the more likely it is to be haunted.

World's Spookiest

SCHOOLS AND LIBRARIES

Are you ready for a ghostly adventure? Then pack up your wits and your **courage**. Let's take a trip to some of the world's spookiest schools and libraries!

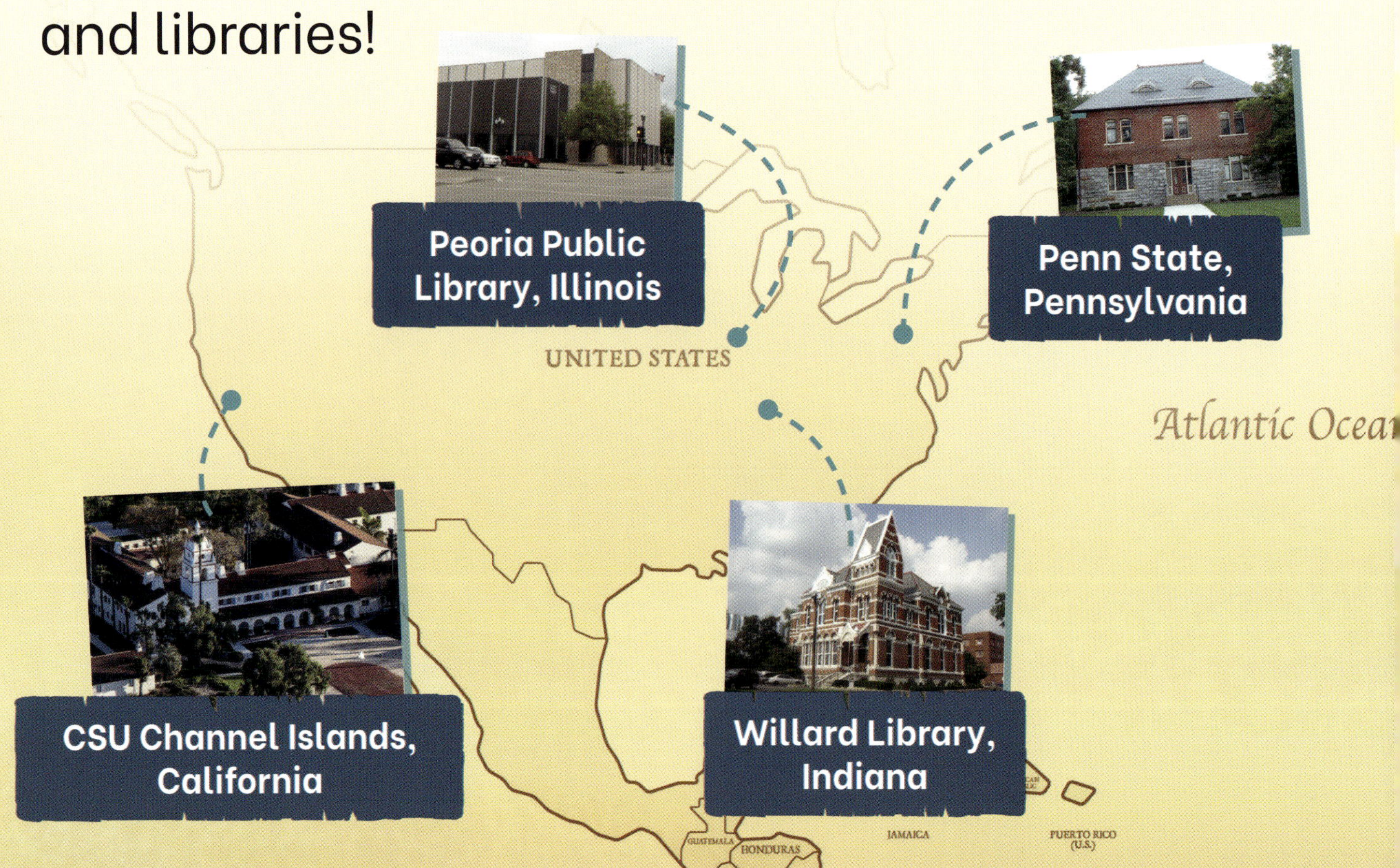

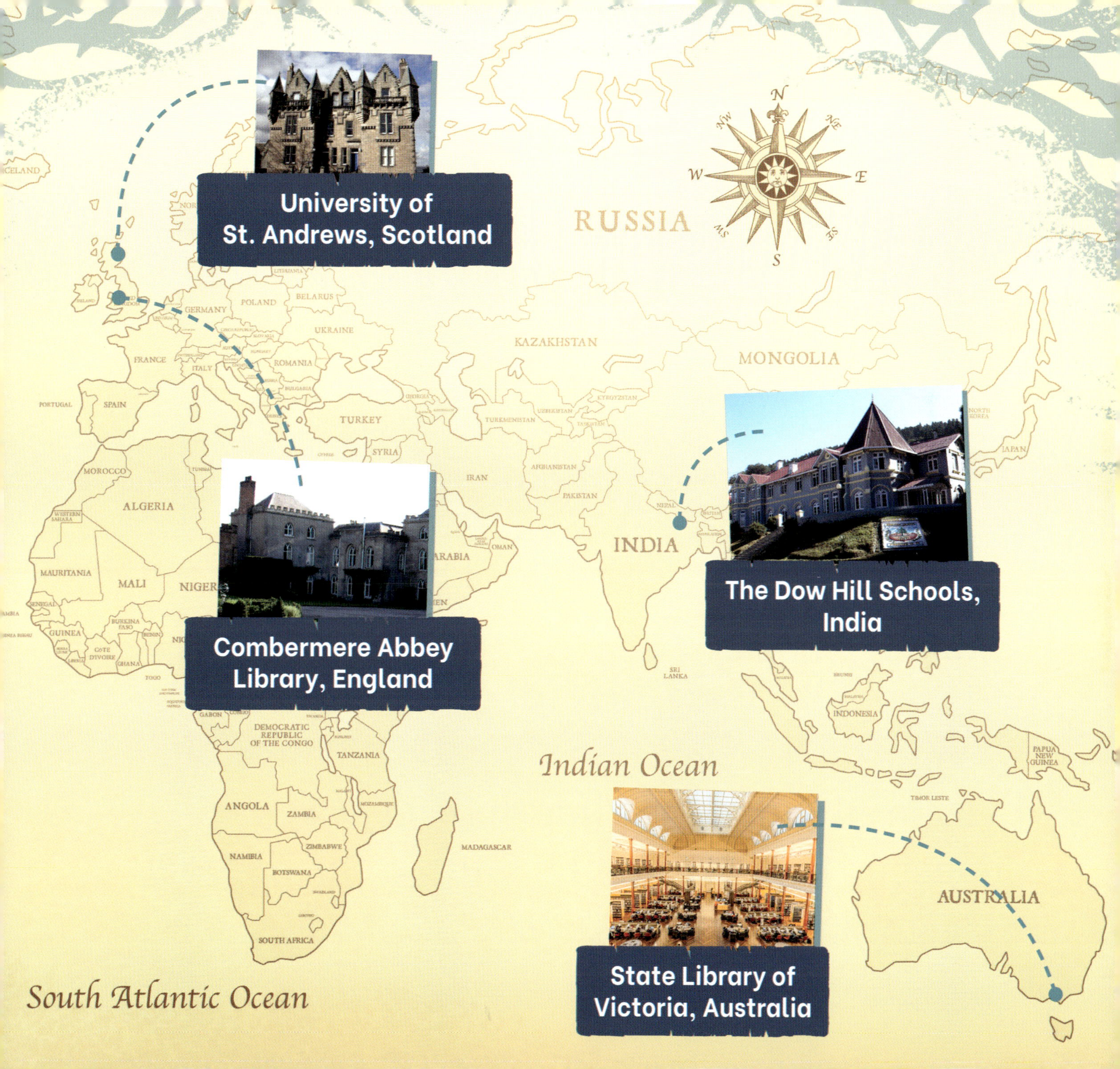

University of St. Andrews, Scotland
Combermere Abbey Library, England
The Dow Hill Schools, India
State Library of Victoria, Australia
RUSSIA
KAZAKHSTAN
MONGOLIA
INDIA
TURKEY
ALGERIA
MALI
ANGOLA
AUSTRALIA
Indian Ocean
South Atlantic Ocean
N
S
E
W

COMBERMERE ABBEY LIBRARY

Spooky stories surround Combermere **Abbey** in Cheshire, England. The abbey is 900 years old. **Legends** tell of **phantom monks**, a ghostly girl, and even a lake monster at the abbey!

The most famous story happened in the abbey's library. In 1891, a **photographer** took a picture in the empty library. Later, she was surprised to see a ghostly figure in the picture. Even stranger, the figure looked just like the second Lord of Combermere. But he had died a few days earlier!

The picture seems to show Lord Combermere sitting in his favorite chair. But at the time it was taken, Lord Combermere was being buried 4 miles (6.4 km) away!

WILLARD LIBRARY

Willard Library is in Evansville, Indiana. It is the oldest public library in the state. It also may be the most haunted! According to **legend**, a ghost wanders through the building.

The library was founded in 1885 by Willard Carpenter. But it wasn't until the 1930s that things got spooky. That's when a **phantom** woman wearing a grey dress was first spotted in the library. People have been seeing the Grey Lady ever since!

Willard Library is a popular location for ghost hunters.

The ghostly sightings aren't the only strange happenings in the library. Bathroom sinks sometimes turn on by themselves. And people claim books and furniture move on their own!

The library holds ghost tours every October. These give visitors the chance to meet the Grey Lady. Some visitors smell a mysterious perfume. Others have felt something brush against them. People report hearing strange noises. Could it be the work of the Grey Lady?

Many people think the Grey Lady is the spirit of Willard Carpenter's daughter, Louise.

THE DOW HILL SCHOOLS

Dow Hill may be one of the most haunted areas in India. **Legend** says it has a haunted forest. Stories tell of ghost children, a headless boy, and red eyes floating in the trees.

The area is also home to the Dow Hill School and the Victoria Boys' School. Many say these schools are just as haunted as the forest around them. People have heard yelling, whispering, and mysterious footsteps, even when the school is closed.

FRIGHTFUL FACT

The city of Kurseong sits on Dow Hill. Many people visit, hoping to see or hear something spooky.

Dow Hill School is more than 100 years old.

CSU CHANNEL ISLANDS

The Camarillo State Mental Hospital in Camarillo, California, was famous for being haunted. It closed in 1997. In 2002, California State **University** (CSU) Channel Islands opened there. But the ghosts may remain.

Students have reported many haunted happenings at the school. They have heard doors closing, people crying, and strange sounds in the walls. Some have reported seeing strange lights, ghostly children, and a **phantom** nurse. There are even reports of a ghostly **patient** in a hospital gown.

Camarillo State Mental Hospital opened in 1936. Many of its original buildings were remodeled for CSU Channel Islands.

UNIVERSITY OF ST. ANDREWS

The **University** of St. Andrews was founded in 1413. It was Scotland's first university. It also may be its most haunted!

One of the university's most famous spirits is that of Patrick Hamilton. He was a former student and teacher. He was burned alive in the school's chapel in 1528.

According to **legend**, anyone who stands where Hamilton died will be cursed. Students have also reported hearing the sound of a fire burning near the spot where Hamilton died.

St. Andrews is the third-oldest English-speaking university.

Other ghost stories are about the ruins of a nearby **cathedral**. Students who go there late at night often report strange sights.

Many students have seen the famous ghost of the white lady. She has long black hair and wears a white dress. **Legend** says the cathedral is also home to a ghostly **monk**. He is said to keep students who visit the cathedral's tower safe.

FRIGHTFUL FACT

According to legend, a **crypt** at the cathedral was opened in the 1860s. There was an open **coffin** in the crypt. A woman with black hair in a white dress was in the coffin.

The St. Andrews cathedral was the largest church in Scotland.

PEORIA PUBLIC LIBRARY

Today, Illinois's Peoria Public Library is a square, modern-looking building. But its everyday appearance hides a dark past.

The property originally belonged to a woman named Mrs. Gray. According to **legend**, she cursed the land. In 1894, the state of Illinois bought the land and built the library.

Since then, people have reported books flying off shelves and mysterious noises. Some have even seen a shadowy figure in the **stacks**. They believe it could be the spirit of Mrs. Gray!

In 1966, the original Peoria Public Library was torn down, and a new library was built where it stood.

PENN STATE

Pennsylvania State **University**, also called Penn State, is known as one of the most haunted US schools! Two of its most haunted places are the **auditorium** and the library.

Students have heard the footsteps of a ghostly **janitor** in the auditorium. In the library, students have felt sudden chills and seen mysterious moving objects. And visitors claim a ghostly figure sometimes moves through the **stacks**!

FRIGHTFUL FACT

People believe Penn State is home to a ghost mule named Old Coaly. Students have heard the sounds of ghostly hoofbeats and braying.

The Old Botany building is one of the spookiest spots at Penn State. Many have spotted the ghost of a woman peering out of the top window.

STATE LIBRARY OF VICTORIA

The State Library of Victoria in Melbourne, Australia, was built in 1856. Since then, many people have worked there. In fact, some may have never left!

According to **legend**, a former librarian named Grace haunts the children's area. A spirit with a **mustache** is said to guard the music room. He's also been known to leave books lying around! People have also reported seeing strange glowing balls of light.

Many spooky sightings have been reported by security guards after the State Library of Victoria is closed.

SPOOKY OR SCIENCE?

You've just learned about some spooky schools and libraries. The creepy stories are fun! But good **explorers** look for reasons for what they see and hear. Strange happenings can often be explained by science.

Do you think the schools and libraries in this book are actually haunted? You might have to visit them to find out!

IMAGINATION

Humans have excellent imaginations. Just hearing about a scary sight can trick your brain into thinking you've seen it too!

CAMERA TRICKS

Old-fashioned cameras, like the one used at Combermere Abbey, took a long time to take a picture. People had to sit very still. If someone moved or left before the picture was finished, it could create a phantom-like image.

EXAGGERATION

Tourist sites may exaggerate spooky stories. They hope this will make more people want to visit.

A TRICK OF THE LIGHT

A glowing ball may seem mysterious. But it usually has a normal explanation. It could be from a camera flash. Or a car headlight shining on a window.

GLOSSARY

abbey – a church that is connected to buildings where nuns or monks live.

auditorium – a large room with rows of seats for an audience to sit in.

braying – the loud, harsh noise made by a donkey.

cathedral – a Roman Catholic church in which a bishop sits.

coffin – a box a dead person is put in before being buried.

courage – strength or bravery.

crypt – a partially or completely underground chamber, especially under a church.

exaggerate (ihg-ZA-juh-rayt) – to make something seem larger or more impressive.

explore – to go into in order to make a discovery or to have an adventure. A person who explores is an explorer.

janitor – a person whose job is to take care of a building, such as a school, library, or hospital.

legend – an old story that many people believe but cannot be proven true.

monk (MUHNGK) – a man who is part of a religious order whose members work and live together.

mustache – the hair that grows on the upper lip.

patient (PAY-shehnt) – a person who is under the care of a doctor.

phantom – an image or figure that can be felt, seen, or heard, but that is not real.

photographer (fuh-TAH-gruh-fur) – a person who takes a picture with a camera.

stacks – an area of a library that has many rows of tall bookshelves.

tourist site – a place people visit while on vacation.

university – a school a student may attend after finishing high school. A university is often made up of several colleges.

ONLINE RESOURCES

To learn more about spooky schools and libraries, please visit **abdobooklinks.com** or scan this QR code. These links are routinely monitored and updated to provide the most current information available.

INDEX

animals 24
Australia 7, 26

California 6, 16
California State University (CSU) Channel Islands 6, 16, 17
Camarillo State Mental Hospital 16, 17
Carpenter, Louise 13
Carpenter, Willard 10, 13
cathedrals 20, 21
Combermere, Lord 8, 9
Combermere Abbey Library 7, 8, 9, 29
curses 18, 22

Dow Hill 14
Dow Hill School 14, 15
Dow Hill Schools 7, 14, 15

England 7, 8
explanations 28, 29

feelings 12, 24
figures 8, 22, 24

ghost hunters 11
ghosts 4, 6, 8, 10, 11, 12, 14, 16, 20, 24, 25
Gray, Mrs. 22
Grey Lady 10, 12, 13

Hamilton, Patrick 18

Illinois 6, 22
India 7, 14
Indiana 6, 10

lights 16, 26, 29

monks 8, 20
monsters 8

Penn State 6, 24, 25
Pennsylvania 6, 24
Peoria Public Library 6, 22, 23
phantoms 8, 10, 16, 29
pictures 8, 9, 29

Scotland 7, 18, 21
shelves 4, 22
smells 12
sounds 12, 14, 16, 18, 22, 24, 28
spirits 13, 18, 22, 26
State Library of Victoria 7, 26, 27

tourism 12, 14, 20, 24, 29

University of St. Andrews 7, 18, 19, 20, 21

Victoria Boys' School 14

Willard Library 6, 10, 11, 12